THE BUG PARADE

THE BUG PARADE

a small book of
poems

BY MS. CAMPBELL

Bains Collier

To my mother who read to me every night,
and to my daughter who listened to me read to her.

Contents

The Bug Parade

In meadows, woods, and gardens bathed
in sunlight's golden glow,
through buzzing, fluttering, and crawling
a bug parade does show.

They march and crawl and eat and drink
they fly and creep along,
a grand procession marches on
of creatures fierce and strong.

The Bug Parade goes on and on
like a brilliant daydream,
made of creatures of many sizes
in lovely endless stream.

At front of our line, a spider
weaving its silk with grace,
eight skillful legs in swift motion
spinning quickly apace.

With its patience and precision
the web's form takes a hold,
a masterpiece of craftiness
a vision to behold.

A long-leg, bouncy grasshopper
so nimble and so fleet,
a great bounding leaper bug to
a rhythmic, joyful beat.

She graces green grassy fields with
agility-bound springs,
a symbol of nature's spirit
a harmonious fling.

Let us not forget the humble
slowly burrowing worm,
digging deep in earthy tunnels
where it wiggles and squirms.

A gardener of deep Earth's soil
a worm plays vital part,
tilling the ground and aiding growth
with its essential art.

From the ants marching steady lines
everyday pavement sight,
to fireflies in the late skies
and twinkling in the night.

In this parading procession
a harmony does thrive,
unveiling the beauty of all
the bugs that are alive.

So let us join this Bug Parade
with excitement and glee,
admiring the bugs around us
in all of their degree.

The Ant's Colony

Inside the bustling realm of Earth
where purpose fills the air,
lives a worker's society
toiling without a care.

It's the ant's living colony
a well-organized might,
building an intricate empire
from early to twilight.

With tiny bodies in motion
march in a perfect line,
carrying burdens with resolve
a workforce so divine.

Their strength is cooperation
as they work all as one,
constructing intricate tunnels
beneath the morning sun.

Gathering food and resources
for the ants to survive,
out of pure love and selflessness
so that they all can thrive.

They communicate using scent
and tactile gestures, too,
the body's language, pheromones
guiding them what to do.

Their tunnels weave a complex maze
a network underground,
a testament to resilience
in depths, no light is found.

They tend to their dutiful queen
she is their existence,
laying eight hundred eggs a day
her labor persistent.

Their society grows and thrives
as they value the whole,
a reminder of unity
working towards their goal.

About Ants

Ants are fascinating creatures that live worldwide, from sandy deserts to lush rainforests. They belong to the family Formicidae, with over 12,000 species of ants! Living in large colonies, ants are social insects that work together as a team.

A single ant colony can house millions of ants, each with a specific job. Workers gather food and build the nest, while soldiers protect the colony from enemies. The queen ant, the mother of all the ants in the colony, lays eggs and is cared for by the worker ants.

Known for their incredible strength, ants can carry objects much heavier than their body weight, akin to a human lifting a car! They use this strength to transport food back to their nest.

Communication among ants is facilitated by chemicals called pheromones. They leave a scent trail that other ants can follow to find food, send warning signals, or help lost ants find their way back to the colony.

Some ant species are remarkable builders, constructing nests several feet tall, while others create intricate tunnels underground. These nests protect the ants from predators and provide a safe place to raise their young.

Ants are incredible creatures with complex social structures and unique abilities. They play a vital role in nature by helping to break down dead plants and animals, which return essential nutrients to the soil.

The Bumblebee's Buzz

Amidst the flowering meadows
where blossoms sway and bloom,
there is a cheerful visitor
a buzz that breaks the gloom.

All the bumblebees are a-buzzing
a gentle, happy sound,
as she shimmies on the petals
spreading pollen around.

With her fuzzy coat of amber
she soars with grace and glee,
collecting flower's sweet nectar
from the blossoms she sees.

Her four wings beat vigorously
in a harmonic flight,
a pollinator in action
bringing nature's delight.

She flits from blossom to blossom
she carries life's embrace,
continually ensuring
floral beauty and grace.

In the golden hues of morning
when dewdrops gleam so fine,
she embarks on her sweet journey
through fragrant intertwine.

Through roses, lilies, and daisies
her dance is like a spree,
a striped ballet on nature's stage
so beautiful and free.

A few shadows mark her return
the meadow starts to dim,
her spirit remains untiring
energy never grim.

Returning home with gold treasures
to her hive before night,
to make honey for family
a golden bee delight.

About Bees

A bumblebee is a large, fuzzy bee that is found all over the world. They are known for their distinctive buzzing sound caused by the rapid vibration of their wing muscles.

The buzz of a bumblebee is unique because it is used to pollinate flowers. When a bumblebee buzzes against a flower, it vibrates the anther, the part of the flower that contains pollen, which is the male reproductive cells of the flower. The pollen is released then sticks to the bumblebee's fur and is carried to the next flower that the bumblebee visits.

Bumblebees eat various things, including nectar, pollen, and honeydew. Nectar is the sweet liquid that flowers produce and is their main food source. Pollen is also a large part of their diet, an important source of protein. Special combs on their bodies collect pollen from flowers into baskets on their back legs. They then take that pollen back to the hive and use it to make "bee bread" to feed to their young. Honeydew is a sugary secretion produced by aphids and other insects, and it is a good source of carbohydrates for bumblebees.

Bumblebees are pollinators and play a vital role in the ecosystem. They help to pollinate many different types of flowers, including fruits, vegetables, and crops. Without bumblebees, many of our favorite foods would not exist.

The Butterfly's Wings

In the garden, she's a whisper
a hushed and silent guest,
she dances on the petal tips
on delicate buds rest.

Her colors speak in a spectrum
a vivid, silent song,
a melody of nature's art
where butterflies belong.

Her wings are transparent and thin
but her beauty so bold,
she's powerful and elegant
as she twirls and she folds.

Yet her wings are but deceivers
who see her as their prey,
the big spots like animal eyes
to make them stay away.

Her proboscis is for sipping
a flower's sweet syrup,
or a fallen fruit or two that
not yet been picked up.

She is a pollen messenger
from nature so divine,
her life is a floral buffet
from bloom to blooming vine.

From a low caterpillar start
to home hanging cocoon,
like magic defies gravity
emerging a winged bloom.

In the grand tapestry of life
she spread threads of pure joy,
a creature of transformation
nature's vivid envoy.

About Butterflies

Butterflies are amazing insects that add a splash of color to our gardens. They start their lives as tiny caterpillars, munching on leaves and growing bigger. When ready, they wrap themselves in a cozy cocoon and take a long nap. After some time, they wake up with beautiful wings and become butterflies!

Their wings are very special. Even though they look thin, they're strong enough for the butterfly to fly and dance from flower to flower. The patterns and colors on their wings aren't just for show; they can help scare away birds and other animals that might want to eat them. Some butterflies have spots resembling big eyes, which can trick predators into thinking they're looking at a giant animal.

Butterflies have a long, curly tongue called a proboscis, which they use like a straw to drink sweet nectar from flowers. They also help flowers grow by spreading pollen from one bloom to another. So, while they're sipping nectar, they're also helping plants!

Watching butterflies is like seeing a little bit of magic in nature. Their incredible journey from crawling caterpillar to graceful, flying butterfly reminds us of how wonderful and surprising the world can be and the beauties of change and life.

The Caterpillar's Leaf

In the meadow's gentle, warm breeze
where sunlight softly gleams,
there rests a hungry traveler
amidst a world of greens.

A caterpillar, small and bright
upon a leaf, it lies,
feasting on the foliage spread
beneath the open skies.

With tiny legs, it ventures forth
in search of leafy treats,
a path of transformation calls
with every bite it eats.

Each stage it grows, a step it takes
towards a grander plan,
until it's time for one last change
as nature's wonders span.

In the cocoon's embrace so tight
away from prying eyes,
the caterpillar reinvents
beneath the azure skies.

As time slips by, both day and night
the metamorphosis ends,
soon, from the cocoon's gentle hold
a butterfly will ascend.

Within this chamber, still and hushed
a secret dance unfolds,
from leaf-bound larva it debuts
with wings like molten gold.

Their wings of hues so vibrant, bright
it flutters into light,
embarking on a vast journey
a most breathtaking sight.

From meadow's heart to sky so vast
this traveler will soar,
a symbol of life's constant change
now free to explore.

About Caterpillars

Caterpillars are the larval stage of butterflies and moths. They are soft-bodied, segmented insects with a voracious appetite for leaves. Caterpillars are found in various habitats, including forests, gardens, and your backyard.

Caterpillars have cylindrical bodies with heads, thoraxes, and abdomens. They have three pairs of true legs on the thorax and up to five pairs of prolegs on the abdomen. The prolegs are not true legs, but they help the caterpillar to grip surfaces and move around.

Caterpillars eat a variety of leaves, depending on the species. Some caterpillars are generalists and will eat a wide variety of leaves, while others are specialists and will only eat a few specific types of leaves. For example, the monarch butterfly caterpillar only eats milkweed leaves.

A caterpillar goes through a series of stages called instars as it grows. At the end of each instar, the caterpillar molts or sheds its skin. After the final instar, the caterpillar pupates. The pupa is a resting stage during which the caterpillar transforms into an adult butterfly or moth.

Caterpillars are important for several reasons. They are a food source for many animals, including birds, spiders, and frogs. They also help to pollinate plants. Caterpillars can sometimes be pests, but they also play an important role in the ecosystem.

The Centipede's Feet

Beneath the moon's silvery glow
in shadows deep and brunt,
the centipede, with stealthy tread
pursues its nightly hunt.

Through twisted roots and fallen leaves
it weaves its silent path,
a spectral dance of mystery
in nature's quiet wrath.

Its many legs, a rhythmic wave
melody in motion,
a creature of the underbrush
master of devotion.

The centipede's feet are agile
twins moving in paired grace,
as it traverses the earth loam
at a furious pace.

Its feet, like delicate brushes
a path of swift alight,
leaving no imprints on the ground
it vanishes from sight.

Its speed is like a lightning strike
with a venomous bite,
ready to catch spiders or worms
or more buggy delights.

It skitters through the forest floor
with fierce fluid motion,
a hunter of the dark midnight
in the night's commotion.

About Centipedes

Centipedes are fascinating creatures that often go unnoticed in the natural world. With their elongated bodies and numerous legs, they move with a unique grace, reminiscent of a rhythmic wave or a carefully choreographed dance. Their many legs, usually one pair per body segment, allow them to navigate through the underbrush and forest floor with agility and speed. Centipedes are primarily nocturnal hunters, using their speed and venomous bite to capture prey such as spiders, worms, and other small insects. Despite their fierce hunting skills, centipedes are elusive and leave no trace of their presence, vanishing from sight as quickly as they appear. They are an integral part of the ecosystem, helping to control insect populations and maintain the balance of nature. Centipedes, with their silent and mysterious existence, embody the intricate and often unseen wonders of the natural world.

The Cricket's Chirp

In the moon-drenched meadow's silence
where blades of grass sway,
resides a small troubadour
a message to convey.

It's the cricket loudly chirping
notes sung proud in the dark,
to serenade a lovely mate
with its enchanting spark.

With wings like delicate parchment
it bangs its rhythmic song,
a chorus of stridulation
that brings their love along.

But chirps aren't only for wooing
it keeps big bugs away,
its mighty bellow deceives
leads would-be pests astray.

Its chirp can warn all the meadow
of coming danger near,
it rubs its forewings together
to warn of danger here.

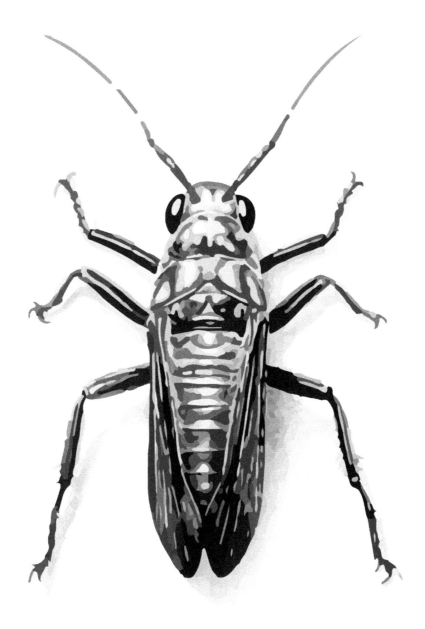

In moonlit fields the crickets thrive
their world a hidden stage,
with each vibration, they create
a song that does engage.

Their legs like fine-tuned instruments
create a rhythmic beat,
in nature's grand orchestral tents
their symphony's complete.

These tiny minstrels of the night
with songs both bold and clear,
remind us of nature's delight
in every chirp we hear.

About Crickets

Crickets belong to Orthoptera, an order which includes grasshoppers, locusts, and katydids. There are over 2,400 species of crickets in the world, and they come in various shapes and sizes.

Crickets are found in various habitats, including forests, grasslands, and homes. They are most common in warm, humid climates.

Crickets are omnivores, which means they eat both plants and animals, including insects, and even other crickets. They have strong jaws for chewing their food.

The chirping sound that crickets make is produced by rubbing their wings together. The rate at which they chirp can vary and be used to communicate with other crickets. For example, male crickets chirp to attract females.

The rate at which crickets chirp increases as the temperature rises. The warmer the temperature, the faster the cricket's wings vibrate. This means that if we listen and carefully count the chirps we can measure the temperature!

The Dragonfly's Dance

On the pond, where lily pads rest
a dragonfly takes flight,
hovers like a helicopter
a sight to see so bright.

With wings of membrane gossamer
she soars through azure skies,
a jewel among the sunbeams
catching insects and flies.

Her four delicate wings unfold
as she leaps with such flair,
moving each independently
to keep her in the air.

She dances with a pure purpose
grace on whispering breeze,
she flies up, down, side or backwards
however she does please.

She is hungry all summer long
mosquitos are her prey,
keeping the population down
eating during midday.

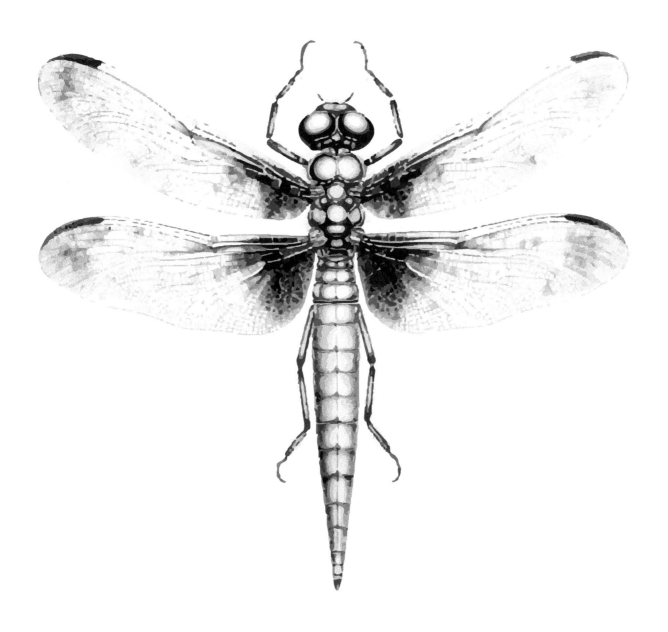

As fast as running big brown bear
when she wants to fly fast,
a wing speed thirty-plus per hour
a blur as she goes past.

They are beautiful and deadly
but their life is so slim,
most live a mere fleeting two weeks
but their brilliance doesn't dim.

With every beat of fragile wings
a short story is told,
a brief span of her existence
a beauty, fierce and bold.

About Dragonflies

Did you know that dragonflies belong to the Odonata order of insects, which includes damselflies? These creatures are well-known for their vibrant, large wings and remarkable flying agility. They can be found worldwide but are most commonly spotted in tropical and subtropical areas.

Dragonflies can live in various habitats, such as wetlands, rivers, lakes, ponds, and forests. Adult dragonflies prefer to live near water because their young, or larvae, reside underwater. Dragonfly larvae are predators and will hunt on the larvae of other insects that lay their eggs in the water, such as mosquitoes. Larger dragonfly larvae will hunt tadpoles, and even small fish. Adult dragonflies are also insectivores, and their flying ability allows them to hunt other flying insects. They are vital to the insect food chain.

The Firefly's Light

Under inky cloak of twilight
where shadows start to creep,
there's a magical spectacle
lighting the dark night deep.

It's the firefly's bright light glowing
brilliant telephony,
they are talking through the darkness
flashing light symphonies.

In the meadows and the forests
amongst the leaves and trees,
fireflies dance in silent rhythms
whispering to the breeze.

Their luminous signals flicker
a language of the night,
a beacon for their companions
in the softened moon's light.

They live in a short summer month
on this beautiful world,
Bringing love, joy, and bright laughter
while they float and twirled.

The flashing lights more than pretty
at a specific rate,
to communicate with others
are looking for a mate.

With fire in name, it would imply
a burning heat inside,
but it is cold within its core
no heat does it provide.

Their gentle radiance enchants
a spellbinding display,
igniting our hope and wonder
as they go their own way.

About Fireflies

A firefly is a beetle that can produce light. It is found in many parts of the world but is most common in temperate and tropical regions. Firefly larvae are carnivorous and eat snails, slugs, and small insects. Some adult fireflies eat other insects, but some are herbivorous and feed on nectar and pollen, and some do not eat anything at all.

Fireflies are bioluminescent, meaning they produce light through a chemical reaction in their bodies. This reaction takes place in special organs in the firefly's abdomen. The light is produced when a luciferin substance is oxidized by an enzyme called *luciferase*. Even though we call them "fireflies," their light produces no heat.

Fireflies use their light for a variety of purposes. The most common use is for communication. Male fireflies flash their lights to attract females. Each firefly species has its unique flashing pattern, which helps the females identify potential mates. Firefly light is also used to deter predators. The light can make fireflies appear larger and more intimidating to predators.

The Grasshopper's Song

In the golden fields of summer
where the warm sun rays beam,
there's a vibrant love melody
carried on an air stream.

Hear the grasshopper's magic song
a lively, rhythmic tune,
rubbing his hind legs and stiff wings
on a June afternoon.

His wings are made of cuticle
are paper thin and strong,
helps him fly up to thirty miles
far all in one day long.

With six legs, two long and four short
he springs into the air,
jumping two feet in a big jump
without a moment's care.

In the dance of emerald blades
where shadows play and merge,
grasshoppers leap in sunlit arcs
in energetic surge.

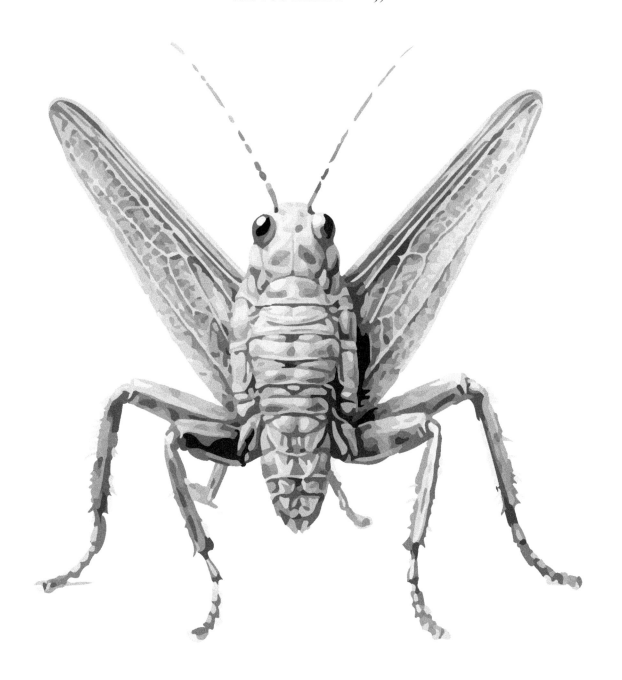

Their bodies beat with the pulse
of summer's vibrant throng,
beating from a long heart organ
running the body long.

As dusk descends with gentle grace
and stars begin their watch,
these acrobats rest their wings
in the night's serene touch.

They hop from plant to blade of grass
an acrobat of zest,
a performer of the meadows
with a song that's so blessed.

About Grasshoppers

A grasshopper is an insect that belongs to the suborder Caelifera. They are among the most ancient groups of chewing herbivorous insects, dating back to the early Triassic period, around 250 million years ago, when dinosaurs first roamed the Earth.

Grasshoppers are typically ground-dwelling insects with powerful hind legs, allowing them to escape threats by leaping long distances. Their other defense from predators is camouflage; when detected, many species attempt to startle the predator with a brilliantly colored wing flash while jumping and (if adult) launching themselves into the air, usually flying for a short distance.

Grasshoppers are *hemimetabolous* insects, meaning that they hatch from an egg into a nymph or "hopper" which undergoes five molts, each time becoming more like their adult form, when they get their wings.

Grasshoppers are plant-eaters, and eat grains, cereals, and vegetables. Some species can become serious pests when they swarm in the millions as locusts and destroy crops over wide areas.

Grasshoppers are found worldwide but are most common in warm, temperate, and tropical regions. They live in various habitats, including grasslands, forests, meadows, and deserts.

The Ladybug's Spots

In garden's vibrant tapestry
where flowers bloom and sway,
there's a polka-dotted marvel
brightening up the day.

It's a bright ladybug with spots
a whimsical display,
she flutters through the foliage
in her charming array.

With wings of scarlet-spotted grace
she dances through the air,
a dainty little deceiver
with spots protecting there.

Her colors aposematic
a fakery hue code,
that dupes her would-be predators
she's a poisonous toad.

She scours on the tender petals
with delicate patience,
feasting on the pesky aphids
under her surveillance.

Her larvae, fierce and hungry beasts
devour pests with glee,
a gardener's tiny ally
in the fight to be pest-free.

With every spot upon her back
a mystery unfolds,
some say it's years of life she'll have
or tales of luck she holds.

In winter, she'll find sheltered nooks
or crevices so tight,
hibernating through the cold
until the spring's warm light.

And when the sun's warm rays return
she wakes from her long sleep,
to lay her eggs on leafy greens
a cycle she does keep.

So next time you see a ladybug
admire her gentle grace,
a tiny guardian of the garden
in her polka-dotted embrace.

About Ladybugs

A ladybug is a small beetle known for its bright colors and spots. They are also known as ladybirds or lady beetles. Ladybugs are found worldwide but are most common in temperate and tropical regions. They live in various habitats, including gardens, forests, and meadows.

Ladybugs have spots as a defense mechanism to avoid predators. The spots, along with the bright color of their body, warn predators that eating a ladybug will result in a nasty and possibly poisonous taste. Most ladybugs have more than ten spots but fewer than 20. The species and genetics of the individual beetle determine the number of spots on a ladybug. More spots develop as they age, but the number is unrelated to their age. Some ladybugs are named after the number of spots they have, like the nine-spotted ladybug, the seven-spotted ladybug, or even the 20-spotted ladybug. The most common species have two, seven, nine, or 13 spots, while some have none!

Ladybugs are beneficial insects because they eat aphids, which are plant-eating pests. One ladybug can eat up to 5,000 aphids in its lifetime! Ladybugs also eat other insects, such as mites, scale insects, and mealybugs.

The scientific name for ladybugs is *Coccinellidae*, and they are so named because of the scarlet color some have. There are over 5,000 species of ladybugs in the world, and they come in various colors, including red, orange, yellow, brown, and black.

Ladybugs have a hard shell that protects them from predators. They also have a pair of forelegs specialized for grabbing and holding prey. Ladybugs use their wings to fly but are not very good at it, usually only flying short distances.

The Monarch Butterfly's Migration

Within the realm of azure skies
where wind whispers its tale,
there's a breathtaking migration
a journey without fail.

The butterfly's sky migration
a wonder to behold,
as they travel across vast lands
a story yet untold.

With dotted wings like painted dreams
they fly with graceful might,
a palette of orange and black
on a canvas of light.

They fly as high as skyscrapers
on bright colors they glide,
embarking on a timeless quest
with nature as their guide.

Driven by an inner compass
they navigate with grace,
covering great 3000 miles
from place to distant place.

They color the world in beauty
as they dance on the breeze,
their presence ignites a wonder
inspiring hearts with ease.

They symbolize transformation
they undergo rebirth,
a reminder of resilience
as they traverse the Earth.

In their spring return migration
find rebirth, hope, and grace,
nature's annual welcome home
in a fleeting embrace.

About Monarch Butterflies

The monarch butterfly, scientific name *Danaus plexippus*, is a milkweed butterfly native to North America. Thanks to its distinctive orange and black wings, it is one of the most recognizable butterflies in the world. Monarch butterflies are known for their remarkable long-distance migration, which takes them from North America to Mexico yearly, covering thousands of miles.

This multi-generational migration begins with the butterflies leaving their wintering grounds in Mexico in early spring. They fly north and east to find breeding grounds, where they lay eggs on milkweed plants. These eggs hatch into larvae, which then transform into caterpillars. The caterpillars feed exclusively on milkweed leaves, ingesting the plant's toxins, which are carried into adulthood and provide a defense mechanism against predators.

Adult monarchs feed on the nectar from various flowers, obtaining sugars and other nutrients essential for their energy needs. The bright colors of their wings warn potential predators about their unpalatable taste, a defense acquired from the toxins in the milkweed consumed during their larval stage.

Monarchs are not only admired for their beauty and migratory feats, but, also play a crucial role in pollination. As they feed on nectar, they transfer pollen from one flower to another, aiding in plant reproduction. However, monarch populations are facing threats from habitat loss, pesticide use, and climate change, leading to a decline in their numbers. Conservation efforts are underway to protect their habitats and ensure the continuation of their incredible migratory journey.

The Mosquito's Bite

In the stillness of the twilight
where shadows softly creep,
there hides a mini blood-sucker
with fangs to make us weep.

She tracks us by our lung's exhale
from thirty feet away,
with cpA-neurons in her body
that help her find her prey.

Only female mosquito bites
an itch we can't ignore,
her long proboscis pierces our skin
with stylets we abhor.

Her jab is spittle and painless
leaving an itch behind,
a reminder of her presence
a little bump to find.

She will thrive in dampened places
where stagnant waters dwell,
a relentless seeker of blood
a painful guest as well.

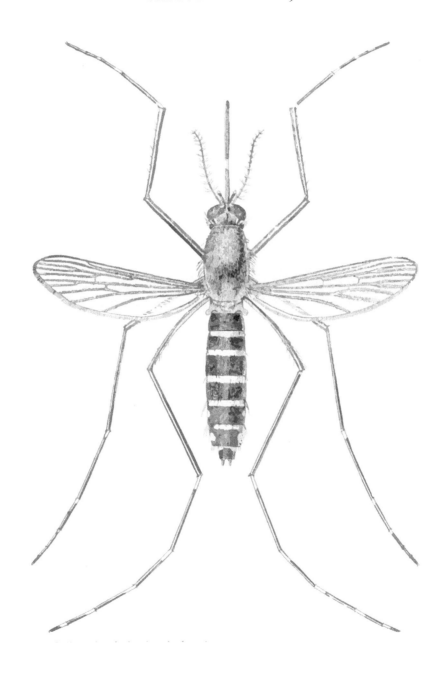

In the hush of evening's embrace
under the moon's soft glow,
she buzzes gliding on air unseen
as the warm soft breezes blow.

With wings that hum a haunting tune
she searches for us her feast,
among the unsuspecting souls
on whom she can unleash.

But knowledge is our strongest shield
against her silent threat,
by clearing pools where larvae breed
we make her path beset.

And with nets that guard our slumber
sprays that keep her at bay,
we protect our soft, tender skin
from her dusk-feeding fray.

Guard against the mosquito's bite
with vigilance and might,
shielding ourselves from intrusion
throughout the day and night.

About Mosquitos

A mosquito is a small, flying insect that belongs to the order Diptera, which includes flies and gnats. The term "Diptera" means "two-wings", highlighting the characteristic pair of wings that distinguishes these insects from other flying insects with more than two wings. There are over 3,500 species of mosquitoes in the world, and they are found in virtually all regions except the coldest, such as Antarctica.

Mosquitoes are infamous for their bites, which can be not only itchy and irritating but also dangerous. The reason mosquitoes bite is that the females require blood to nourish their developing eggs. In contrast, male mosquitoes do not bite and instead survive on nectar and plant juices.

The process of biting is not actually performed with teeth but with a specialized mouthpart called a proboscis. This long, thin structure is capable of piercing the skin much like a needle. Once inserted, the mosquito uses the proboscis like a straw to draw blood from its host. The saliva of the mosquito contains anticoagulants, substances that prevent the blood from clotting, ensuring a steady flow of blood for the mosquito to feed on.

It is important to note that mosquito bites are more than just a nuisance. They can be a significant public health concern as mosquitoes are vectors for various diseases, including malaria, dengue fever, Zika virus, and West Nile virus. These diseases can have severe impacts on human populations, especially in areas where healthcare resources are limited. As a result, controlling mosquito populations and preventing bites are critical components of public health efforts in many parts of the world.

The Moth's Flame

In the still of the dark night sky
where lights soft embers trace,
a delicate four-winged creature
flits through the night's embrace.

A moth is drawn to burning flame
to find the mate it needs,
or maybe just confused by light
or a yearning to feed.

Her wings of protein called chitin
covered by tiny scales,
they are light and thin but strong wings
in a lofty spring gale.

While their cousins, the butterflies
who are beauty-renown,
go looking for one and a moth
more likely will be found.

They can eat fallen fruit from the
high branch overhead,
but be careful when you're biting
you might find larva instead.

Silk that's used in neckties or scarfs
have a moth origin,
we use their spun, strong silk cocoon
to make fabric for them.

Moths do aid us in many ways
so watch for them with care,
flitting through the night's gentle hold
nature's symbol they bear.

About Moths

Moths are fascinating creatures that often go unnoticed in the shadow of their more colorful relatives, the butterflies. These nocturnal insects are an integral part of the ecosystem, playing various essential roles in maintaining ecological balance. With their delicate four-winged bodies, moths navigate the night sky, drawn to light sources. This attraction to light is a behavior that has puzzled scientists for years. Some believe it is an instinctual search for a mate, while others suggest it could be a misguided quest for food or a simple confusion caused by artificial lighting.

Moths possess wings made of chitin, a protein that provides both strength and lightness, allowing them to flutter effortlessly through the air. These wings are covered in tiny scales that give moths unique patterns and colors. While butterflies are often celebrated for their beauty, moths are equally diverse and fascinating in their own right. They can be found in many environments, from lush forests to urban gardens, and are more likely to be encountered at night than butterflies due to their nocturnal habits.

Moths also play a crucial role in plant pollination, as they feed on nectar and, in the process, transfer pollen from one flower to another. Some species have even co-evolved with specific plants, making them vital for the reproduction of those species. Additionally, moths serve as a food source for various other animals, including bats, birds, and other insects, thus contributing to the food web.

Silk production is one of the most remarkable contributions of moths to human society. Certain species of moths, particularly the silkworm moth, are cultivated for their silk cocoons, which are harvested and spun into silk fibers. This luxurious material is used in various products, from clothing to home furnishings.

In conclusion, moths are more than just nocturnal insects attracted to light; they are vital contributors to natural ecosystems and human economies. Their presence in the night sky reminds us of the intricate connections that exist in nature and the importance of preserving biodiversity for the health of our planet.

The Praying Mantis's Prey

In the silent realm of shadows
where patience finds its home,
there's a vigilant observer
a hunger that's well-known.

It is the praying mantis' prey
a tale of stealth and might,
it waits among the foliage
for a moment to strike.

Its prey are small garden bugs that
we see as insect pests,
like flies, crickets, moths, grasshoppers
mosquitoes and the rest.

Their raptorial legs designed
to not let go of prey,
with power superhero strength
it'll never get away.

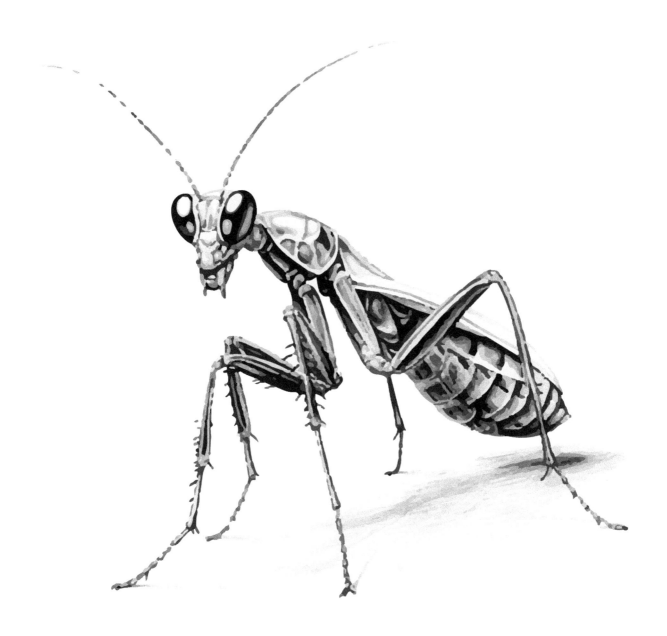

The mantis strikes with lightning speed
its mouth a swift demise,
an insect does not have a chance
when hunger in its eyes.

Let us marvel at its prowess
in nature's ancient play,
a mantis is a predator
within the grand array.

About Praying Mantises

The praying mantis is a fascinating and formidable predator in the insect world, embodying the perfect blend of patience and precision. These insects are known for their unique appearance, with their elongated bodies, triangular heads, and prominent front legs folded in a prayer-like posture. But don't be fooled by their serene stance; praying mantises are skilled hunters, masters of camouflage and stealth.

In the silent realm of shadows where patience finds its home, the praying mantis waits motionless among the foliage, blending seamlessly with its surroundings. Its prey, often minor garden bugs such as flies, crickets, moths, grasshoppers, and mosquitoes, remain unaware of the lurking danger. These pests, which we often regard as nuisances, form the bulk of the mantis's diet, making it a natural ally in pest control.

The praying mantis strikes with astonishing speed. Its raptorial legs, designed to grasp and hold onto prey, are equipped with sharp spines to ensure that the victim has little chance of escaping once caught. The mantis's strike is so swift that the prey is often subdued before it realizes what has happened. This combination of speed and strength is akin to a superhero's power, showcasing the mantis's prowess as a predator.

The praying mantis's role in nature's ancient play is awe-inspiring and crucial for maintaining ecological balance. As predators, they help control populations of other insects, preventing overpopulation and the spread of pests. Their presence in gardens and agricultural fields is a natural form of pest control, reducing the need for chemical pesticides.

In conclusion, the praying mantis is a marvel of nature's design and an essential player in the ecosystem. Its predatory skills, patience, and stealth make it a fascinating subject of study and an invaluable ally in the garden. As we marvel at its prowess, we are reminded of the intricate and interconnected web of life in which the praying mantis plays a vital role.

The Spider's Web

In darkened corners of the world
where shadows gently creep,
there's a master weaver lurking
spinning fear as you sleep.

It's the spider's web construction
so light and delicate,
she crafts her intricate design
with silk from spinnerets.

Her threads, like glistening silver
catch water in the air,
a testament to her patience
in nightly weave affair.

She spins her sticky, silken strands
with artistry and grace,
she makes seven kinds of silk lines
each for different case.

She drinks from the morning dewdrops
adorning her design,
as sunlight turns her sturdy web
into jewels that shine.

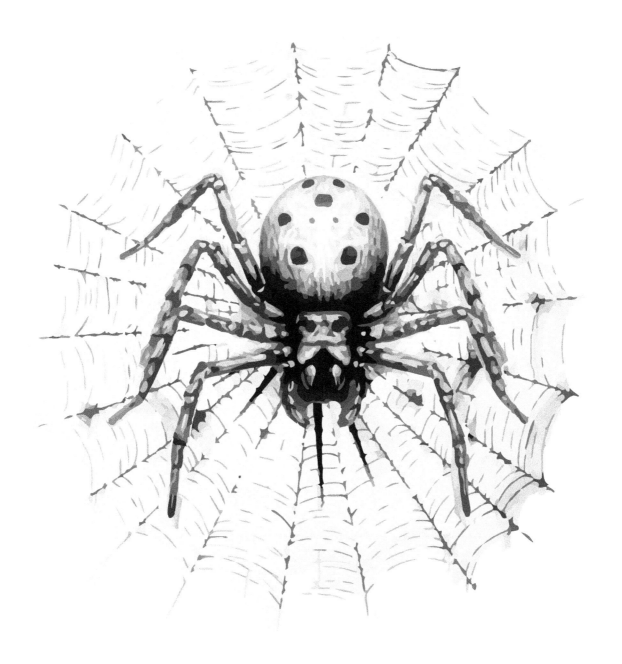

A fortress of her survival
where prey becomes ensnared,
she bites then wraps it up
never to be shared.

So let us marvel at her craft
with wonder and respect,
acknowledging her place
in nature's intricate connect.

For in the spider's web
we glimpse the interconnected whole,
a reminder of the beauty
that emerges from each soul.

About Spiders

Spiders, often misunderstood creatures, are master weavers of the natural world. In the quiet, darkened corners, where shadows gently creep, these skilled architects work tirelessly, spinning webs of intricate beauty and remarkable strength. The construction of a spider's web is a marvel of nature's engineering, showcasing its ability to craft a delicate yet durable structure from silk produced in its spinnerets.

The spider's silk is a wonder, with threads that glisten like silver, capturing water droplets from the air and turning the web into a shimmering masterpiece. This silk is not only beautiful but also incredibly versatile. Spiders can produce up to seven types of silk, each serving a specific purpose, from constructing the web to wrapping up prey. The sticky strands of the web are a testament to the spider's patience and artistry as she spins gracefully, creating a trap that is both a home and a hunting ground.

As morning breaks and dewdrops adorn the web, the spider's creation is transformed into a stunning display of jewels that shine in the sunlight. Yet, this beauty is not just for show. The web is a fortress of survival, where prey becomes ensnared, allowing the spider to secure a meal. With a bite and a wrap, the spider ensures that her catch is never to be shared, demonstrating the efficiency and precision of her hunting skills.

The spider's web is more than just a home or a hunting ground; it is a gateway to the world, a testament to the strength and resilience of these creatures. It is a story of survival, spun from the essence of the spider's being. As we marvel at the craft of these master weavers, we gain a deeper appreciation for their role in nature's intricate connection. The spider's web serves as a reminder of the interconnectedness of all life, highlighting the beauty that emerges from each soul, no matter how small or misunderstood.

The Termite's Mound

In the heart of dark, dense forests
where secrets dwell unseen,
stands a towering testament
a marvel to be seen.

It's the tiny termite's big mound
a fortress wrought with care,
as they build their ancient empire
ten feet into the air.

Their tiny jaws are relentless
they will toil day and night,
crafting intricate dark chambers
a labyrinth of might.

Inside their dark earthen kingdom
a complex world unfolds,
filled with nurseries and chambers
where life's story is told.

With intricate ventilation
a system wise and sound,
they regulate their tall home's heat
with airflow abound.

Their mound, a vertical masterpiece
made from dirt, spit, and poop,
millions of termites hard at work
like a fast army troop.

Termites are in many places
including underground,
in fell dead trees and mighty stumps
and wooden structures found.

They shape their world with a purpose
each member plays a part,
making intricate skyscrapers
a living work of art.

About Termites

Termites, often hailed as architects of the insect world, are small, pale-colored insects known for their social nature and organized colonies that span across the globe, from lush tropics to temperate zones. With over 3,000 species, termites display a range of forms and functions, from winged to wingless varieties, all encased in a protective exoskeleton. Remarkably, termites are constantly active, as they do not require sleep, dedicating every moment to their colony's survival and expansion.

Their architectural feats are most notable in the Southern Hemisphere, where termite mounds serve as both marvels of engineering and vital ecosystem components. These structures offer protection, food storage, and space for colonies to thrive. Termites have a unique digestive system with specialized microbes to decompose cellulose, allowing them to feed on various plant materials and play a crucial role in ecological balance.

The construction of termite mounds provides a stable environment for the colony and enriches the surrounding soil, enhancing its fertility. Some mounds are so significant that they become natural landmarks. Through their intricate mounds, termites demonstrate their architectural skills and essential role in environmental health, promoting soil aeration and nutrient cycling. The world of termites is a testament to collaboration, innovation, and environmental stewardship, offering valuable lessons in nature's intricacies.

The Worm's Tunnel

Beneath us in earthly layers
where secrets intertwine,
there lies a hidden architect
in tunnels, it defines.

With a slender, wriggling body
it delves with steady might,
creating intricate pathways
while hiding in plain sight.

Its purposeful excavation
enriching soil's embrace,
a tireless worker of the Earth
nutrients in its trace.

It aerates the farmer's dark loam
as tirelessly it churns,
creating fertile growth pathways
where life can take its turn.

It feasts on decaying matter
recycling Earth's decay,
transforming organic remnants
pooping along its way.

As it journeys through the darkness
it treads with humble grace,
it breaths and exhales through
its skin into soil space.

Let's honor the small worm's tunnel
in its unending quest,
acknowledge its contribution
at nature's soil behest.

About Worms

Worms, often overlooked as mere wriggling creatures beneath the earth, play a crucial role as hidden architects of the soil. With their slender, elongated bodies, worms delve into the earth with remarkable efficiency, creating intricate pathways that significantly impact the environment. These pathways, or tunnels, serve various purposes, from aerating the soil to facilitating the movement of water and nutrients. As worms move through the soil, they consume organic matter, breaking it down and enriching it with essential nutrients.

One of the most critical functions of worms is their ability to aerate the soil. As they burrow, they create spaces that allow air to circulate, promoting the health of plant roots and other soil organisms. This aeration is particularly beneficial in agricultural settings, where it can enhance soil fertility and improve crop yields. Additionally, the tunnels created by worms provide channels for water to penetrate deeper into the soil, preventing surface runoff and erosion while ensuring that plants have access to the moisture they need to thrive.

Worms also play a vital role in the recycling of organic matter. As they feed on decaying plant material and other organic remnants, they break down complex molecules into simpler forms that plants can easily absorb. The waste produced by worms, commonly known as worm castings, is rich in nutrients and serves as a natural fertilizer for the soil. This process of decomposition and nutrient cycling is essential for maintaining the health of the soil. As worms journey through the darkness, they breathe through their skin, exchanging gases with the soil environment and further contributing to the soil's vitality.

The humble worm's tunnel is a testament to the creature's unending quest to enrich and sustain the soil. By acknowledging the contributions of worms to the natural world, we gain a deeper appreciation for these small but mighty architects of the earth. Their tireless work ensures the continued fertility and health of the soil, supporting the growth of plants and the overall balance of ecosystems.

The Wasp's Sting

In the blue skies of buzzing wings
where tension fills the air,
there lives a fearless warrior
with weapon sharp and rare.

The wasp's sting is deadly and sharp
an attack to reckon,
it defends its nest with venom
no option to beckon.

With a sleek and slender body
it hovers on command,
an agile flying predator
its stinger in demand.

With bright yellow stripes so vivid
warning of a danger,
a fierce guardian of its queen
and alert to strangers.

Bees sting only once, then they pass
defending their own hive,
but wasps can live past many stings
while still they stay alive.

Venom contains a message scent
it's called a pheromone,
the urgent smell tells other wasps
they must defend their home.

If you see a wasp with stylet
it has to be a ringer,
because it is female, not male
they don't have a stinger.

In nature's delicate balance
it carves its rightful space,
building nests with thin, papered walls
a sanctuary place.

Though its sting may bear discomfort
it teaches us a truth,
respect boundaries and keep out
a lesson from your youth.

About Wasps

In the bustling blue skies, the wasp emerges as a fearless warrior equipped with a rare and sharp weapon. The wasp's sting is a defense mechanism and a deadly tool used to protect its nest and colony. This insect is known for its venomous sting, which it uses to fend off predators and intruders. The venom is potent and capable of causing significant pain and even allergic reactions in some individuals. Unlike bees, which can sting only once before dying, wasps can sting multiple times, making them formidable defenders of their territory.

The wasp is characterized by its sleek and slender body, often marked with bright yellow stripes that warn of potential threats. This vivid coloration signals other animals to stay away, indicating the presence of danger. Wasps are agile flyers and efficient predators, with their stingers always ready for action. They are fiercely protective of their queen and the hive, always alert for any signs of intrusion. The venom of a wasp's sting contains pheromones, chemical signals that alert other wasps to the presence of a threat, prompting them to defend their home.

Wasps play a crucial role in nature's delicate balance. They build their nests from a paper-like material, creating thin-walled sanctuaries that house their colonies. These structures are marvels of natural engineering, showcasing the wasp's ability to construct and maintain a safe environment for its kin. While the sting of a wasp may cause discomfort, it serves as a reminder of the importance of respecting boundaries and the natural world. The wasp's presence in ecosystems is a testament to the intricate relationships among different species, each carving out its space and contributing to the overall harmony of nature.

The Water Beetle's Swim

In the shimmering ponds and lakes
where insect life resides,
lives a floating navigator
with legs that gently glide.

It's the water beetle's swimming
a dance on the surface,
as it strides on water's surface
with elegant purpose.

Its long, thin, sinewy hind legs
rows the water with grace,
a master of aquatic realms
gliding from place to place.

Beneath the moon's soft, silver glow
in waters deep and clear,
the beetle is a keen hunter
where prey should rightly fear.

Its mandibles ready to clasp
on unsuspecting meals,
tadpoles, snails, larvae, or small fish
to its hunger, they yield.

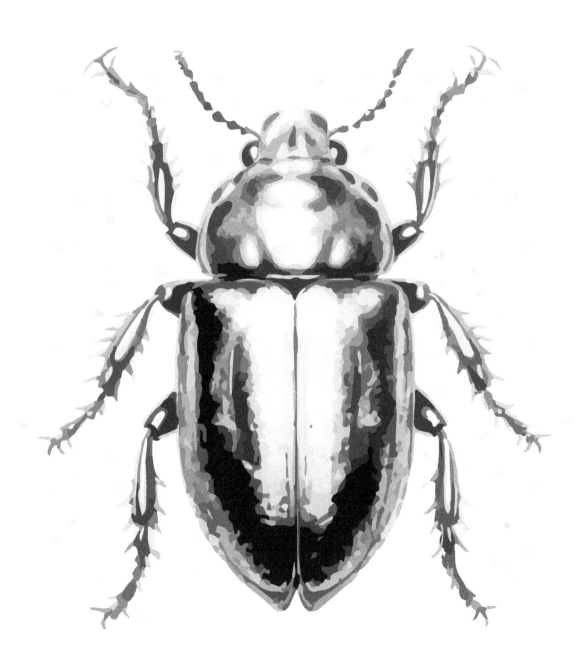

Yet not all feast on flesh and shell
some find their joy in green,
shredding leaves, or eating algae
in a world rarely seen.

From egg to larva, then pupa
a transformation grand,
until pop, an adult emerges
to take its final stand.

There's one generation per year
in life's relentless flow,
some live three years beyond their birth
in the waters below.

Beware the giant among them
a bite that sears like fire,
yet fear, not its painful greeting
for it harbors no ire.

Through seasons change, it perseveres
beneath the sun and moon,
a tiny voyager of the depths
its symphony, a tune.

About Water beetles

Water beetles are a diverse group of over 4,000 species of aquatic insects, ranging from predators to herbivores. They vary in size and shape, with adaptations for swimming or walking along the water's bottom. Depending on the species, their diet includes other insects, small fish, tadpoles, and aquatic vegetation. The life cycle of water beetles consists of four stages: egg, larva, pupa, and adult, with most species producing one generation per year.

These beetles are well-adapted to their aquatic environment, using long, fringed hind legs for swimming and exhibiting a range of colors, typically black or brown. While some aquatic insects can spend their entire adult lives underwater, beetles have different breathing mechanisms. It's worth noting that giant water bugs, a type of water beetle, can deliver a painful bite if disturbed, though it is not considered medically dangerous.

The Water Boatman's Legs

Beneath the tranquil pond's facade
where ripples gently sway,
lives a creature of the water
who's quick to get away.

Their strong legs are miraculous
a marvel of design,
as it propels through liquid realms
with legs slender and fine.

Its legs, delicate hairy oars
are shaped like a small scoop,
this adaptation helps them to
on the water to scoot.

He will serenade the lilies
in a whispered nocturne,
rubbing their ridge legs to their heads
to make a chirping turn.

Water boatmen are oval
elongated in shape,
with a big, broad head and large eyes
to see all the landscape.

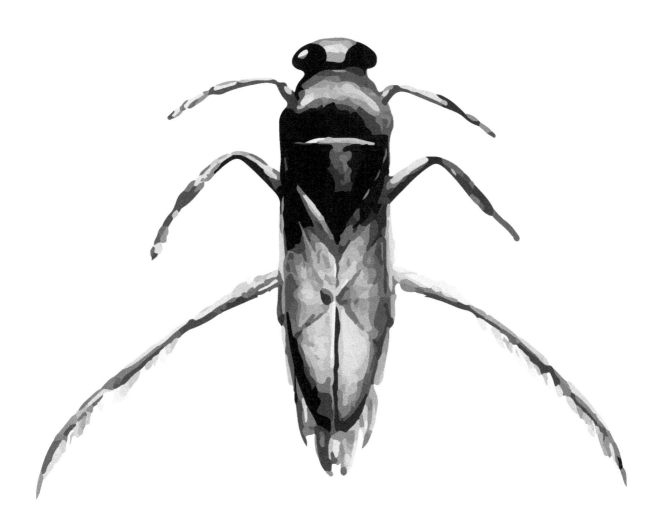

In ponds and lakes on edges they dwell
beneath the moon's soft beam,
eating algae in strict silence
inside life's quiet stream.

No threat to man, nor beak's bite
they will feed, chirp, and roam,
controlling pests all night along
in their own water home.

Observe the water boatman's legs
with wonder and delight,
appreciating its prowess
in the water so bright.

About Water Boatman

In the magical world of freshwater ponds and streams, there lives a tiny, adventurous creature known as the Water boatman. These little insects are quite the explorers, paddling through the water with their long, oar-like hind legs covered in special hairs. These hairs are not just for show; they create a bubble of air that makes it super easy for the Water boatman to glide through the water with the grace of a skilled swimmer.

Water boatmen come in many shapes and sizes, but they all share a love for the water's calm and the lush vegetation that grows there. With their shorter front legs, they hold onto plants as if hugging their favorite teddy bear. But don't let their peaceful nature fool you; these creatures are mighty hunters, feeding on small aquatic animals with long, straw-like mouthparts. They're like underwater superheroes, keeping the waterways clean and balanced.

Despite their fierce hunting skills, Water boatmen are gentle giants to humans. They don't bite and prefer to spend their nights foraging the muddy bottoms of their watery homes for algae and tiny organisms. Sometimes, they even help control mosquito populations by munching on their eggs and larvae. Some male water boatmen are also known to be quite the musicians, creating chirping sounds by rubbing their legs together and adding a soundtrack to their aquatic adventures.

So, next time you're near a pond or a slow-moving stream, take a moment to look for these fascinating creatures. Water boatmen are not just insects but paddlers, hunters, and musicians of the water world. They play an essential role in the ecosystem and remind us of the wonders beneath the surface.

The Whirligig Beetle's Dive

On the pond's shimmering surface
where ripples gently play,
lives a beetle with dive prowess
in a captivating display.

They breathe on deep water dives
with homemade scuba gear,
using trapped air on their stomach
diving without a fear.

Its vision has dual purpose
to see top and below,
it spies approaching predators
in the water they'll go.

Our beetle is a strong back-swimmer
belly-up, upside-down,
backstroke Olympic medalist
whose strokes are world-renown.

They cruise from surface to bottom
stirring up muck to find,
tiny algae and plants to eat
or larvae would be divine.

In the whirligig beetle's dive
we find some enchantment,
a reminder of the beauty
in the world's advancement.

About Whirligig Beetles

A whirligig beetle is a small, predatory beetle found in freshwater habitats worldwide. It is characterized by its flattened body, which allows it to swim easily on the water's surface. Whirligig beetles have two pairs of eyes, one pair adapted for seeing above the water and one pair adapted for seeing below the water. This allows them to see prey from above and below the surface, giving them a significant advantage in hunting.

Whirligig beetles are also known for their ability to swim in circles. This is a behavior that is thought to help them to confuse predators. When a whirligig beetle swims in circles, it is difficult for a predator to track its movements.

Whirligig beetles may dive to escape predators, to find food, or to lay their eggs. When a whirligig beetle dives, its flattened body creates a pocket of air around itself. This allows it to breathe underwater for short periods.

About The Author

Ms. Campbell is a seasoned writer whose passion for storytelling has spanned various genres and formats. Her journey as an author began with a deep love for words and a keen interest in capturing the essence of human experiences through her writing. Over the years, Ms. Campbell has authored a cookbook, plays, and articles, each piece reflecting her unique perspective and creative flair.

Ms. Campbell's writing career is a testament to her versatility and dedication to the craft. Her books cover many topics and audiences, but she finds a special joy in writing for children. The innocence and wonder of childhood serve as a powerful inspiration for her poetry, where she skillfully weaves together vivid imagery, rhythmic verses, and engaging narratives. Her poetry not only entertains but also educates and inspires young readers, fostering a love for literature from an early age.

Born in New Jersey and raised in Los Angeles, Ms. Campbell has experienced the rich cultural diversity of the United States. For the past 20 years, she has made Washington, D.C., her home, a city whose vibrant cultural and historical tapestry has significantly influenced her writing. This environment provides endless inspiration and a deep appreciation for diverse perspectives. Ms. Campbell's educational background is equally impressive, with extensive studies in writing, literature, and psychology.

Ms. Campbell's personal experiences also play a crucial role in shaping her work. Living with multiple disabilities, she brings an authentic voice to resilience, empathy, and inclusion themes. Her advocacy for disability rights is evident in her writing, where she strives to promote understanding and acceptance. Ms. Campbell's storytelling often reflects her belief in the power of words to create change and build bridges between people.

Beyond her professional achievements, Ms. Campbell is a devoted community member. As a former Girl Scout leader and dedicated volunteer, she has consistently demonstrated her commitment to service and leadership. These experiences have enriched her writing, infusing it with values of cooperation, perseverance, and kindness. Fond memories of catching fireflies in the backyard with her child and numerous trips to camping sites have added a layer of nostalgia and wonder to her poetry. Her involvement in scientific studies during Girl Scouting trips has further fueled her curiosity and passion for exploration.

Ms. Campbell currently resides in Washington, D.C., where she continues to write, inspire, and connect with her readers. Her latest venture into children's poetry is a heartfelt project that she hopes will bring joy and imagination to young minds. Through her poetry, Ms. Campbell aims to spark curiosity and a love for reading in children, encouraging them to explore the world of literature with open hearts and minds.

When she's not writing, Ms. Campbell enjoys practicing French, cooking, and spending time with her beloved community. Her life's journey, marked by both challenges and triumphs, is a testament to her un-wavering spirit and dedication to her craft. Ms. Campbell invites readers of all ages to join her on this literary adventure, where every poem is a doorway to a world of wonder and possibility.

Printed in the USA
CPSIA information can be obtained
at www.ICGtesting.com
LVHW080224110824
787898LV00005B/55

9 798989 126408